DOTS & DASHES

Crab Orchard Series in Poetry
Open Competition Award

DOTS & DASHES

POEMS BY **JEHANNE DUBROW**

Crab Orchard Review &
Southern Illinois University Press • Carbondale

Southern Illinois University Press
www.siupress.com

20 19 18 17   4 3 2 1

The Crab Orchard Series in Poetry is a joint publishing
venture of Southern Illinois University Press and *Crab
Orchard Review*. This series has been made possible
by the generous support of the Office of the President
of Southern Illinois University and the Office of the
Vice Chancellor for Academic Affairs and Provost at
Southern Illinois University Carbondale.

*Editor of the Crab Orchard Series in Poetry: Jon Tribble
Judge for the 2016 Open Competition Award:
Maura Stanton*

Library of Congress Cataloging-in-Publication Data
Names: Dubrow, Jehanne, author.
Title: Dots & dashes / poems by Jehanne Dubrow.
Other titles: Dots and dashes
Description: Carbondale : Crab Orchard Review
& Southern Illinois University Press, 2017. |
Series: Crab Orchard Series in Poetry
Identifiers: LCCN 2016058056 |
ISBN 9780809336098 (softcover : acid-free paper) |
ISBN 9780809336104 (ebook)
Subjects: | BISAC: POETRY / General.
Classification: LCC PS3604.U276 A6 2017 |
DDC 811/.6—dc23
LC record available at https://lccn.loc.gov/2016058056

For Jeremy

War feels to me an oblique place.
                    —*Emily Dickinson*

the dear sound of your footstep
and light glancing in your eyes

would move me more than glitter
of Lydian horse or armored
tread of mainland infantry
                    —*Sappho*

CONTENTS

PLEASE STAND BY

A CATALOGUE OF THE CONTENTS
OF HIS NIGHTSTAND

One orphaned oak leaf from his uniform.
Loose change. A pair of collar stays. A tube
of mentholated chapstick going warm.
An accordion of ancient Trojans, lube
that's meant to tingle when it touches skin.
The leather cuff he bought in Santa Fe.
A sample of cologne that smells like gin,
cigars, and prohibition, the satin sway
of bodies in a sweating room. A card
his mother sent—she wonders when he'll write
again. A tin of peppermints now hard
and powdery as chalk. A tiny light
he aimed at shadows as we lay in bed
(bright spheres) until the battery went dead.

READING POETRY ON MARYLAND PUBLIC RADIO

As a poet where's the anti war? . . . interview seemed
grievously war enabling and shallow.
> —online comments section, May 2010

Two days from now, my voice will be so gone,
        my next interview
                will be taped
in dots and dashes, bits
          of poems spliced
to make one unbroken
                      communiqué.
Right now, I'm trying not to answer when
I'm asked about my husband's latitude
        and longitude,
               because I can't recall
what the Navy thinks
              is need-to-know,
so that I end up saying something like,
He's somewhere in the middle of the sea,
        as if he's stranded in
            a ten-foot dingy
from a story by Stephen Crane.
                  In fact,
I'm hoping not to get my husband fired,
        because unlike a book
            of poetry,
this radio has reach
           and audience,
and even if my words are small currents
        they're traveling, perhaps
                to where he is—
I haven't heard him speak
               in four months,
and when I learn, a year from now,
that phones were possible, that any time
        he could have dialed me from the ship,
           I understand
distance is a place
               some people love

like the site where land
                          becomes a line
vanishing, deep water
                          the only view.
And now I'm being asked
                    about nakedness,
the page not far from the blank-
                                    white open
                    of the bedsheet,
in that they're both a space for what's impolitic.
                    And if my poem
hasn't done enough—carried signs or made a peace march
                                    on the Capitol—
it's because five months from now
          my husband's coming home,
                                    and depending on
the weather or the day,
                    we'll talk or not
about the next shipwreck,
how soon we'll both be overturned by this.
                    Or as Crane writes,
the problem with the ocean is the waves,
          that beyond the first there lies
                                    another, waiting
to do something *in the way of swamping boats.*

[TO A NAVY WIFE, IN MARYLAND]

Some say cruisers, others carriers
cabled to catch descending bodies,
and some will argue for destroyers,

those barbed surfaces that pierce
oceans and air. I say whatever
can come home will be the vessel

of desire. Is not the Aegis
Combat System—a warning made
of electricity, tined waves of sound—

named for a shield Athena wore
when she was angriest, and therefore
beautiful, the golden scales of it

like snakes writhing? The uninitiate
would think the goddess hurricane.
So, to the husband gone, although

you're slow in your returning,
you do at last return, filled now
with all the same mythologies,

the seabag dropped by the door,
the coat you shrug off a kind of shield,
how it smells of animal and salt.

RAMROD

Perhaps I wanted an officer, only I thought I said a man,
but sometimes transmissions have a way of breaking

      at the place one needs precision most of all,
so that whoever read my message at the other end,

put in a form for officer when all I asked for was a man—
the gap between what's right and what is written

      like a squad's request for more white pills
and the metal pails delivered weeks from now.

Instead of a man, I received a regulation figure,
stern and straight from the box, gilded at the insignia,

not to be touched for its brightness, so shined
      it was best to leave the actual thing

standing at attention on a shelf, the little spine
gone ramrod—a device, I learned, once used to shove

the bullet down a barrel, to tamp the powder,
      to guarantee the spark at the peak of battle,

when the infantryman could barely hold the musket
steady. Ready aim fire. Cruel to consider

the body an instrument, the tool it could be,
how easily it entered common speech—sometimes

the ramrod sat unpurposed, heavy enough to serve
      as paperweight or to prop a lazy door.

Perhaps I should have specified a gentleman,
but what was the point? Everything belligerent

      looked the same—the gun, the cannon.
When I watched the officer sleep,

I could see, divested of his uniform,
      how he remained rifle and cartridge.

And I learned that some collect these things—
the ramrod restored, the one a soldier

carried with him to the Civil War.
Imagine the fumbling hand. The officer lay so quietly

      I could mistake him for a beautiful antique
which, if I didn't value, I understood that others did.

And so I kept him out of sentiment. Displayed him.
Impressed my guests with this curiosity from a field

we'd only read about—the dust, the sweating horses,
      the quick, iambic marching of the boots.

CADETS READ "HOWL"

Gordon Ball, February 1991,
Virginia Military Institute

All seven men are shaved-to-bone, heads bare
and bending toward the page, each page the same,
the same white cover edged in black, each square,
made parallel. They sit inside the frame
of class or study hall and read their books.
What's here—lined paper and pencils capped
with pink erasers. What's here—these looks
of uniform intensity the camera snapped.
But though they're nearly duplicates, I keep
returning to the one curled forward in
his chair, elbow on table, half-asleep
perhaps or simply bored, not quite the twin,
his body the most readable, leaning—
yet like a text that won't give up its meaning.

OFFICER CANDIDATE SCHOOL

For years the letter hung on your wall,
framed to show both sides beneath glass,

the first with its quick sortie into cordiality,
the other severing whatever truce remained.

Later you described when it first came
Gunnery Sergeant waved it like a flag,

the surrender asked of you, that moment
when he read my message to the barracks

full of men, all of them sitting on the deck
and shining brass. It's the practice

in such places to search for contraband.
Once, a girl sent you pictures of her tabby cat,

the joke that *Schwab got pussy in the mail.*
I've always been skilled in the strike

that language makes on sentiment.
Long after this, you spoke about those weeks

in Pensacola when you uncreased
my letter from your pocket, reread it as a drill,

like the callusing of feet in combat boots,
how you loved that dispatch for the precision

of its cruelty, my words and their marching
orders to leave me the fuck alone.

A GLOBAL FORCE FOR GOOD™

Please take a seat.
There is a slot for you
        at home and over-
seas—a ship, a crew,
                a port of call.
Sign on the dotted lines
        to rocket-launch,
to dive, to sweep for mines.
        Report for work
in every hemisphere.
        A signing bonus
for that extra year.
                Accelerate
your life, full speed ahead.
        A man without
a mission's better dead.
        Handle the truth,
a gun, the cruiser's wheel.
        Become as hard
and rare as tungsten steel.
        Be Maverick.
Be Goose. Be G.I. Jane.
        Be water capped
with white. Be hurricane.
                Initial here
and here. Let's cut your hair.
        Let's uniform
the body that you wear.
        Let's see what whisky
we can commandeer.
        Please take this T-shirt
as a souvenir.
        Please take this pen,
this bundle of brochures.
        You are the Navy
now. The now is yours.

USS RONALD REAGAN

When my husband says the aircraft carrier
he's headed to is named for Ronald Reagan,
that actor from our childhood TV screens,
matinee idol who called America
a kindly, greening land, and Washington
a shining city on a hill, I say
is everything Ronald Reagan? To say
it's just a ship, an aircraft carrier,
is to ignore that everywhere in Washington
he is—the airport now is Ronald Reagan,
the metro stop. Throughout America
are elementary schools and mega-screens
in stadiums named *him*. Sometimes the screens
flicker a final score. Sometimes they say,
we will not be deterred. America,
they say, achieves its destiny. The carrier
navigates waters of forgetfulness, like Reagan
himself, I think. Those years in Washington,
did he imagine himself George Washington
when, reading off the teleprompter screens,
he spoke of duty, freedom, strength? Reagan,
the great communicator, who liked to say
that facts are stupid things. On the aircraft carrier,
they eat jelly beans that taste like America,
the pucker of sour apple, America
of plastic licorice. In Washington,
I think of my husband sent to the carrier,
how soon he will be staring at those screens
which stutter white with information. He'll say
all is quiet on the *Ronald Reagan*—
and how I'll want to believe, although Reagan
could never persuade me that America
was steering toward a flat horizon. Say
there's sin and evil in the world and Washington.
Let our banner proclaim on all the screens
a victory. The aircraft carrier,
I say, is in deep ocean, Ronald Reagan
an aircraft carrier, a man, an America.
And Washington, a million static screens.

SOMETHING CHARMING

*I heard Bullets whistle and believe me there was
something charming in the sound.*
> —George Washington, in a
> letter to his brother, 1754

Years later, the President explained,
If I said so, it was when I was young.
At twenty-two, his joy was unrestrained—
so this was war. And though the shots had sung
for him, the hollering of cannons fired,
the quavering of lead as it shrieked by,
well soon the singing stopped or he grew tired
of the tune. He watched his soldiers die.
At Valley Forge, he wrote about the men,
naked and starving as they are, their feet
gone bloody in the awful snow. Again
he asked for blankets, shoes. Again the sleet
fell everywhere, uncharming in its sound—
those frozen, stinging voices all around.

ACHILLES

We remember the hero angry in his tent.
It's like this at the start of any war,
when diplomacy is done and politicians say
embargoes are for kicked dogs,
no man revered for signing treaties.
The soldier tires of the undented shield.
And all the weapons in the world desire hands
that know how to wield them.
We need not have sat on the warrior's cushions
at the edge of the paused battle
while hate was a cup of wine he downed,
to know how helplessly the wind murmured
in those weeks, fate a stone that wouldn't be budged.
All night, Achilles practiced dropping his sword
like a man letting go of his lover, the terror
in him what most of us feel when stripped, alone.
Each time we turn the page, we hope he won't return
dressed in the intimate armor of his rage,
behind him the dead future of the sea
and the plain dark up ahead. We whisper to him,
don't go. The poem is already written—
like the senators who went to desert countries
and said we would be welcomed as victors
freeing slave-girls from their chains.
Later, unfastened at last from his own fury,
Achilles must have sought the arrow-point,
have lunged for it in longing,
revealing the small mortality of his heel.

OLD GLORY

You watched it flap on its mast.
                It jittered in the rain,
thwacking against the side of itself,
        all night, a wet refrain—

ka-thump as it strained the cord
           and buckled in the wind
while your neighbor ignored the clang
              of a thing undisciplined.

The U.S. code requires
        a spotlight on the flag.
And it shouldn't be torn or crumpled.
        And it shouldn't drag

on the ground, though you saw
           your neighbor drop it,
leave a mudprint on the corner.
        You called out to him—
                    stop it.

In fact, you said nothing.
        Your neighbor's blinds were drawn,
and the stars unthreaded
        on his patriotic lawn.

TACKLE BOX

From the weight of it,
  the way its contents clicked and rubbed
  with a sound like artificial wings,

one would have thought my husband
  a collector of silken miniatures,
  hand-tied flies for catching fish.

But inside were the insignias of his work—
  pins in the shape of oak leaves,
  shoulder boards, ribbons,

oceans of obedience
  in those shipshape compartments.
  And, watching him search

for a ceremonial medal,
  it was easy to imagine he was looking
  for a nymph or minnow, blue

damsel or yellow sally,
  as if gone to war
  were the same as Gone Fishing.

And when he found the gold length
  of braid or the sleeve device
  and lifted it from the box,

he was like a man who loves
  those still Sundays on the water
  and could already picture his line

far over the edge, cast out,
  a green deceiver knotted at the end,
  waiting for something to happen.

CAUTION: HOLE IN SHIP

In dry dock the cruiser floated

feet above the deck—

like a model leviathan

I once saw

in a hall of natural sciences—

so that a grown man

could walk full underneath

without dipping his head

to clear the keel.

Someone had strung

crime-scene tape

across a hatch left gaping,

posted a sign

to stop workers falling

the way children

used to fall down wells.

For weeks my husband peered

into the gap,

as if it were the eyepiece

of a microscope

so sharp it could reveal

the small interior of cells.

Later, when the *San Jac*

was sealed up

and returned to water,

he stole the cardboard square.

It sat in his stateroom

all through the next deployment,

sliding a bit

on those nights of high alert,

when the sea

was streaked with foam.

CAUTION:

HOLE IN SHIP.

The man I didn't understand

was this one—

who could think each day

about the thin hull

that held the ocean out—

                not when I could barely stare

at the plaster diorama

                        of a squid

wrapped around a whale—

                embrace so much like love

or longing

                    —those terrible bodies

drifting in their blue,

                        uncertain light.

WHAT WE TALK ABOUT WHEN WE
TALK ABOUT DEPLOYMENT

Jane explains that deployment is the blizzard dumping feet of snow
on everything and one unbroken shovel in the world. Beth says I've
sat through six, which makes me a professor in the field of absentol-
ogy. Mary calls deployment a vacation from desire, her hands gone
reaching nowhere else. I say deployment is misfortune—you only
care when it's your own. Jane tells us about the time water filled the
light above her bed. Turns out the air conditioner was on the fritz,
that drop by drop it leaked into the globe of glass. Deployment, like
sleeping underneath a small aquarium alive with electricity. Beth
talks about the wife from some long poem who waited twenty years,
can you imagine, twenty years, before her husband finally dragged
his wandering back home. Mary likes the space created by a single
dinner plate. Other deployments, I say, bore us as much as other
people's dreams retold. Speaking of which, Jane dreams the washing
machine is spinning frozen margarita mix—her whites turned lime
and triple sec. She gets drunk on hanging linens out to dry. Beth
dreams that every book contains a hall of blinking mirrors. I only
see myself, she says. What Mary dreams is one enormous couch, ex-
tending infinite across a room, where she can stretch her legs forever
and never touch another body. I dream the four of us are talking.
I can see the separate narratives our mouths have formed. I can see
how we keep trying to change the subject—what about the weather,
we say, what about the lonely shadows of the afternoon, how when
we speak of it, December almost seems to disappear.

MUCH TATTOOED SAILOR ABOARD USS NEW JERSEY

LCDR Charles Fenno Jacobs, December 1944

i.

Squint a little, and that's my husband
        in the photograph, the sailor on the left—
the one wearing a rose composed of ink
        and the Little Bo Peep who stands
before a tiny setting sun and the blur
        on his forearm, which might be a boat—
while the sailor on the right is leaning in,
        his fingers touching the other man's skin,
tracing what looks like the top of an anchor
        or the intricate hilt of a sword, perhaps
wiping blood from the artful laceration,
        in his other hand something crumpled,
his cap I think or a cloth to shine brass,
        lights on a bulkhead, fittings and fixtures,
because let's not forget this picture
        must be posed, the men interrupted—
mops laid down, ropes left uncoiled, or else
        on a smoke break, Zippo and Lucky Strikes
put aside—no war for a moment, only
        the men bent at beautiful angles,
a classical composition this contrast
        of bodies and dungarees, denim gone black
and their shoulders full of shadow—
        although on second thought how effortless
this scene, both of them gazing toward
        a half-seen tattoo so that we too lean in
trying to make out the design on the bicep,
        close enough we can almost smell the erotic
salt of them and the oil of machinery,
        which is of course the point, as when in a poem
I call the cruiser's engine a pulse inside my palm
        or describe my husband's uniform,
ask him to repeat the litany of ships and billets,
        how one deployment he sliced himself
on a piece of pipe and how the cut refused
        to shut for months—*Hold still*, I tell him,
I need to get the exquisite outline of your scar.

ii.
My husband in his new ink, the blade
                of his shoulder
        now unfamiliar for its anchor,

is a text I visit with my fingers.
                Overseas,
        an artist has tattooed him

with the start of a tiger—three sittings
                I'm told it will take
        to make the teeth glisten.

Still healing, he turns his back to me
                in the bedroom,
        and says, *it hurts*, and waiting

for my response, he anticipates a touch
                that says,
        you do this to yourself.

It's always like this for our bodies. I too
                have a bramble
        of blackberry and blossom on my back.

What postcard from another
                place. What
        permanence. What coiled machine

like a clicking pen. For my husband,
                each design
        introduces some new story,

a mermaid's turquoise tail, a ship
                sinking
        on his arm. Come home,

he would no matter what be strange.
                Consider the tiger:
        half-finished leaf and shadow.

My husband as well to me is bare
        contour, a sketch
     that takes the shape of intimacy.

He's also crouched in the tall leaves
        of my thinking,
     his eyes waiting to be shaded in.

iii.
Even in war,
the artist's narrow

seeing finds an aperture
to let in light across

the injuries of skin.
Our appetite is keen,

Sontag says, for pictures
of bodies held in pain,

elemental satisfactions.
The swallow flitting

on a collarbone
is still a wound,

however deliberate
in its position,

the symbolism clear—
that like birds we return

to violated shores,
that we love ourselves

for flinching, that we
love ourselves more

when we refuse to look
away from the hurt

a needle makes, the first,
fine point of red.

THE SIGNAL FLAG

For every letter of the alphabet,
there is a flag that spells things out, phrase
by phrase, whole messages in stark displays
of stripes and checkered squares and crosses set
on seas of white. For every flag, a threat
that's near—*steer clear of me.* So many ways
to warn of danger in the world, to raise
alarm. *Man overboard. I've lost my net.*
If only marriage came equipped with signs
as manifest, a flag that says *I'm drowned,*
that says *I'm trying to communicate.*
It would be easy then to read the lines
and circles, not to run the ship aground,
to change one's course before it is too late.

[THE DEPENDENT SAYS]

Be kind, and if you ask
why I wear the soot
and shadow of a widow,

my sleeve torn at the seam,
a certain sleeplessness
around the eyes, don't

be surprised when I answer
Aphrodite, who offers up
desire then deploys

          the beloved
so distant out to sea
he might as well be drowned.

CALLING ANY STATION

FROM THE PENTAGON

He brings me chocolate from the Pentagon,
dark chocolates shaped like tanks and fighter jets,
milk chocolate tomahawks, a bonbon
like a kirsch grenade, mint chocolate bayonets.
He brings me chocolate ships, a submarine
descending in a chocolate sea, a drone
unmanned and filled with hazelnut praline.
He brings me cocoa powder, like chocolate blown
to bits. Or chocolate squares of pepper heat.
Or if perhaps we've fought, he brings a box
of truffles home, missiles of semisweet
dissolving on the tongue. He brings me Glocks
and chocolate mines, a tiny transport plane,
a bomb that looks delicious in its cellophane.

DRONE

We will see small drones that deliver wedding cakes.
—"Drones Over America," *60 Minutes*

a bee a buzz a monotone
    a drone that hummingbirds
across a town a drawler
    a crawler of cities
on an instrument
    a string that moans drone
of panoramic pix little clicks
    emitted in the sky sleek
robotic fly that whirs its wings
    bringer of things that blast
and boom to pass away
    drag out as if all living plays
slo-mo gizmo that spins
    through smoke
to the burning trees below
    device at the meltdown ghost
in the walls and hills and halls
    of the Capitol storm drone
and parrot airdog gone aerial
    a body that's flown remote
by a land-bound god finder
    of those who would stay
unfound subject of research
    searcher of subjects lurcher
that jets a box of sugared tiers
    to the church in the nick
of time to shoot
    the vows wrest the guests
from their facelessness zoom
    toward the bride and groom
drone of white noise
    and beak unveiled
as if to speak now and forever
    hold the peace

RUNAWAY MILITARY SURVEILLANCE BLIMP DRIFTS FROM MARYLAND TO PENNSYLVANIA

The aerostat looks less like a balloon
than like a woman, her body's milky curves—
        she trails her mooring lines all afternoon.
Untethered, cutting loose, she feints and swerves.

        She's carried farther north, while on the ground
news cameras film her progress through the air,
        her seeming reluctance to be earthbound,
reclining on the breeze as if aware

        she's wanted, as if she feels the fervor of
the fighter jets that follow close behind.
                Perhaps surveillance is a kind of love,
she thinks, the interest of an ardent mind.

        And when at last her cables snag the trees,
she's dragged, sinking from the clouds, beautiful,
        submissive as a woman on her knees,
whose power lies in acting dutiful.

[WHEN I MARRY EROS]

He's dressed in the uniform
of war, our wedding photograph
a shot of cream and navy,

the blue he wears so dark it's black.
Already we are turning from
the camera, and between us

a window curtained on the world.
How quickly the outside
clatters in. Soon I'll watch him

give a sharp salute, the shape
his hand creates against the sky
a missile aimed at something high.

HOMEPORT

Even on weekends the cruiser
      would shudder, flicker spaces
            with a redorange blink,

then a gasket crack or a valve stick shut
as if by weather or malicious hands,
            the engine room home

     of all catastrophe.

           I would stretch and reach
across the bed to find furrowed sheets
where my husband had slept until 3 A.M.,

when he answered the captain calling,
      whose perpetual fury machine
was the only system that never broke,

and my husband would yessir to him
who was steamingmad on the ship,
before slipping into the chill of coveralls,

the blueblack uniform of service,
      which in a certain light
           had the confining fit of love.

MY HUSBAND CALLS ME SHIPMATE

to indicate
        the rank
and file of
        my mistake,
the way under-
        way he names
some dumbass
    sailor bozo
who left
        the valve open
which should
        be shut, who
forgot to hit
        the switch
no matter
        that the drill
remains
    the same each
time, each time
        the same
routine of click
        and flick,
the color-coded
        flag to signal
danger, safety,
    or something in
between—says
        broke-dick,
clusterfuck—says
    negative to mean no,
which is to say
        that language
of the engine
        room has no
shut-off, no
        blinking light
to let the user
    know that this

is not the place
    for Private Fubar
if you please
      —says *roger that*
although there is
    no radio, no
Roger in the room—
    says will comply
although he won't
    —says shipmate
although no mating
    now, this bed
not ever made
      into a ship.

FIVE POETRY READINGS

i. United States Naval Academy

I'm talking
             to a thousand
uniforms in a stadium
                         that's meant
for contact sports or four-star
                                    silver speeches.

My words return
                 in blurred, metallic waves,
so that it's hard to hear
                         myself
above the sound of me, this tinny,
                                    tiny version,

as if
      I'm listening to a distant me
reverberate,
             fathoms I say of marriage,
the darkness wide,
                     percussive as a mine.

How young
           the plebes all seem,
laughing when I say
                    fuck,
and afterward, in line
                        for autographs,

they ask
         about my wedding ring,
how much it cuts
                 the skin,
the kind of bruise commitment
                                leaves.

Their collars gleam
                with golden anchors.
Already they're weighed
                down. I tell them *light*,
I say, *you'll barely feel the burden*
                     of this thing.

ii. Dodge Poetry Festival

Circled by our strange company
            of veterans and poets
preparing to read is the great,
golden silence of a dog, Sadie Mae,
            who all day has leaned
at her owner's side, guided
through crowds on a thick line of rope,
and now, has placed herself
at the heart of everything,
            a furred focal point
toward which all our voices aim.
            Later, in the strafed light
of the stage's wings, she lies
near a curtain, unstirred
            by shots of applause.
Her coat seems to muffle
our perplexing human sounds.
            We stroke her muzzle,
so unlike the violence of that word—
it lifts at the clatter of poems,
before resting again on the ground.

iii. Andrews Air Force Base

I spot him right away,
                          the pilot rigid
in his flight suit, still zipped from crotch to neck—
all of him sealed and insular
                          —arms crossed,
until at question time, his hand
                                        shoots up
no doubt like one of the planes he flies
too fast I bet,
                          so that his wife worries
about this need to push the edge of speed
and sound, so that she can't stop
                          cleaning,
stop dragging the stringy mop across the floor,
or streaking the Windexed glass
                                        with disquiet.

I hate this guy. He hasn't said a thing yet,
but I know what's coming,
                          the sentences
that soar on wings of certainty—I've met
his type before.
                          Later, when I watch
the video, I can see it on my face,
a smile meant to disarm
                                        hostilities,
my best defense in moments such as these.

It's terrible and lonely and difficult,
I say, meaning
                          I think to be married
to a man like him or any of the men
in this room—or for that matter,
                                        my husband—
who've sworn to protect against threats foreign
and domestic,
                          against poems perhaps,
those tiny detonations made of words.

iv. Walter Reed National Military Medical Center

The poem is not
a body, although

enjambment comes
from the French

to put a leg across,
each sentence twisted

at the break.
The sterile rooms

through which we wheel
are called stanzas.

And what are words?
—prosthetics made

to bear the weight
of what is lost,

the improvised blast
at the volta

which is another way
of saying turn.

v. Naval War College

I can't stop watching the other
                dependent in the room—
        she's coral
                in a sea of khaki,

my gaze dragging back
                to the bright reef
        of her dress
                each time I look up from the page.

I've just read a poem about loneliness,
                how two people
        are a distance measurable
                like the nautical miles between ships,

and now I'm reading a sonnet,
                also it seems on the theme
        of so much water,
                though rhyming this time,

because it's best when one is lost
                to look for echoes,
        navigate by stars
                resembling other stars.

This isn't the first time
                I've found myself
        speaking to the only spouse in a crowd
                of officers, as if we're always pulled

to what's familiar,
                both of us trying
        to determine our places relative to land.
                She's nodding now. And I believe

we've reached the same conclusion,
                that reference points

keep moving out of reach,
　　　that when I say vessels

I mean boats and bodies,
　　　that there's no more imperfect union
　　than marriage
　　　　or the marrying of words.

PATTON

My husband loves to stand before a giant flag
that isn't there and quote the General
to his troops, which is to say to me,
that I'm the troops who need rallying
before the beach is stormed, or in our case,
before the combat of routine marriage.
All Americans love to fight, he says.
The sting of battle is the sting of coming home.
Husband-and-wife is killing business.
We must love one another by the bushel-
fucking-basket. He says, an army is a team.
You're not all going to die, he says,
although the bed may seem a rendezvous
with the enemy. But that's the goddamned thing.
Only sons of bitches give in to cowardice,
purple-pissing their separate lives
while heroes fling themselves against a coast.
This we'll defend. Every bastard is afraid
of waking beside the same body every day,
the way she lies there like a corpse,
and you think to yourself, how long must I stay
in this shell hole, the hell with that.
But then, she moves, and you wipe the dirt
from your face and you realize this is the victory.
To wait it out. Only a sock full of shit
decides to run. Rip open the belly of wedlock.
Make the screaming your best friend,
make a constant advance on the line, make
it blood and gut, a thousand consecutive hours
of lousy commitment. Breed bravery
in yourself until the bullet in your lungs
becomes a triumph, and thirty years from now
you'll tell your grandson this wheeze
and cough is how to recognize a man.
All right, you wonderful guys, go grease
the treads of your tanks, he says. That is all.

POEM

Understandable in a single, rapid reading and generally
free of errors in grammar, mechanics, and usage.
—U.S. Army Writing Assessment Form, 1009W

When my husband writes this POEM
(Personal Observation Encased in Metaphor)
he tags the text with color-coded flags
to guarantee the safety of the crew.
            This line is flammable.
This line can spit high-pressure steam.
What happens next in this POEM
depends on weather or geopolitics or
the Commanding Officer who's hoping for
another star.
            This POEM believes in clarity,
the precision of a hard left turn,
the need for evasive action to avert collision.
Above all else, logic and significance.
When my husband writes this POEM, all passages
are cleared of objects that interfere.
He checks the temperature of engine parts.
He enters all formations in a log.
      In my husband's expert hands,
this POEM can dock without incident,
having reached its stated goals of breadth
and depth.

NOVEMBER 11

My mother calls it pushing and contractions,
not Armistice or Veterans,
or according to the Internet, the day

Sherman began his burning
to the sea. Riots broke out in Tibet.
On this date, Kurt Vonnegut was born,

and the Internet lists him first
as soldier, then author, academic,
the order perhaps not incorrect,

given *the smell of mustard gas
and roses*. After a bombing, what
do the birdies say with their barbed-

wire beaks? On this day: a battle,
a massacre. A thing called disaster.
Vonnegut wrote of the present—

how wide it was, how deep.
The doctrine of transubstantiation
was defined on this day, the way

Vonnegut said of blood in the snow,
the color of raspberry sherbet.
My father calls this one of his happiest—

the bread he consumed, the wine.
The sudden transformation of a man.
The Internet tells me: on this day

the end of occupied France.
And if I trust Vonnegut, we're *trapped
in the amber of this moment,*

this date and any other fossilized,
suspended in resin, held dying
and delivered in the hard yellow light.

AT THE READING OF THE ANTIWAR POETS, 2007

Someone says, we're living through an age
the ancient Greeks would understand,
internecine,

                  unrepairable as red
ceramic shards. The famous poet calls
the soldiers babykillers, says fuck them.
It's time to resist the lyrical, she says,
to write as if

                        on fragments of papyrus.
In all the poems, everyone is marching
to protest some piece of news
among the monuments. All the dead
are marble in their sleek, heroic poses.

I think of the summer when we drove
the famous poet to the airport,
my husband out of uniform

                        but undisguised,
not like Odysseus returning as a beggar
to his home. I remember how he held
the door for her and how they debated
Plato's warring

                horses of the soul
and how I met my husband in a class
on Ovid where we learned longing
changes us

                    to limestone, or causes us
to caress the white bull—no matter
that he's animal and his child minotaur,
the divided

                offspring of our love.

COMBAT VETERAN LIVES HERE PLEASE
BE COURTEOUS WITH FIREWORKS

Fourth of July lawn signs for veterans with PTSD

Our weekend brings its long barrage—the flare
and cherry bomb, the snap, the thunder-flash.
A rocket streaks the sky. Green mortars crash.
A roman candle lacerates the air
with sparks, a hissing brilliance everywhere
that wrenches shadows from the grass. Each splash
of light sets off the dogs—they smell the ash,
they scurry from the missile's steady glare.
Small parachutes drift paper-frail as thought.
There's smoke, a shattering of shells, a crack
which sounds the way a rifle might when shot
into the night. Our neighborhood is hot,
alive with waiting, one moment powder-black
then bright, as if we're all under attack—

FROM THE ABERDEEN PROVING GROUND

After the blast, the geese return
        to pecking at a razored field,
beaks like tweezers teasing
        shrapnel from a wound.
All spring, the sound has hurled
        kilometers across the Bay to us,
as much a form of local color
        as the sharp striations
of a Smith Island Cake,
        or a waitress in the diner saying Hon.
We barely notice each gun
        and ordinance gone off,
the way we hardly see
        the colonial charm of High Street,
the tall ship at the waterfront
        with its gleaming portholes
to the eighteenth century.
        Only when those guests
from out of town arrive,
        come to demolish a regional dish
like the salted purse of shad roe
        or rockfish caught in Rock Hall,
do we again pick out the boom
        and after-boom, the dust
of silence that for a moment
        falls on everywhere we look.

[AS FOR THE SAILORS]

You find peace like a woman,
difficult to endure
for more than a few days,

her hands expert in the ways
of pouring wine, of smoothing
down the sheet. But soon,

all things become monotony.
She's lovely, yes, her voice
a wind that wiffles on and on.

The backward curving of her spine
when she is perched above,
reminds you of the shape

that water makes as it departs
the shore. It's time to leave—
no rocking body better than a boat,

no booze a substitute for the lurch
of storms, a world that tilts
with such indifference

you only want to stare
the tempest in its hollow eye
and know that it returns the dare.

THE ALARM

At 4 A.M. your cell phone rings awake—
the alarm is set to a sonar's ping,
as if we're sleeping underwater, a lake
of sleep, a sea of it. Slowly you bring
your hand from underneath the weight of sheets
and blankets, fumbling to stop the sound
from finding our positions, how it repeats,
repeats it seems for hours. We're always found—
as in the movie where the submarine
lies so submerged it stays unseen, unknown,
until a neon blip across the screen
confirms there's something there. You grab the phone
at last and hit the snooze—five minutes more
to dream about the little pulse of war.

OVER

SOS

Distress is signaled by a run of threes:
three dits three dahs three dits, and then it all
begins again. The meaning of this call
for help can be discerned in its reprise.
No matter where the listener starts, the pleas
for help—*please help me please*—repeat their small
alert. The ship is threatened by a squall.
The ship is lost, has suffered casualties.
If we are ships we too have signaled land
or called each other in the dark. We've scanned
the sky for help. We've said *emergency*,
a sequence made of silences and tones.
And when it ends, we've said *seelonce feenee*.
The sea says nothing back. The anchor groans.

[THEN THE GOD OF WAR]

Bragged that he could drag off
my husband in a metal box,
which in his hands would be

more toy than new technology,
a plastic warship in a rising tub,
and Ares a toddler climbing in,

splash of bubbles, soap, bashing
together boats. What little brunt
it takes to sink a floating thing.

A ROW OF RIBBONS

They're laid in lines,
         on plastic backings,
                  so many stripes of service,

thick horizontals,
         fine verticals that signify
                  campaigns, as if duty

could be turned to strips
         of variegated braid.
                  Some are studded

with metallic stars—
         pierced, we might say,
                  with longing for the celestial,

perpetually remote.
         Gold and silver, bronze,
                  and all of it unreadable

to civilians—
         except as a cordoned-off
                  achievement.

To us they're only rules
         and bars of color,
                  each one a regulated streak

of a body belonging
         to a greater one.
                  But ask my husband,

and he'll point to awards
         on his chest, which are
                  to him an ocean,

or a certain sea
         where his ship
                  once swept for mines.

What if these were enough
          for the widow, the mother
                    of the suicide—who,

presented with medals,
          would frame them
                    beside a folded flag,

touch these things
          until they became more
                    than grosgrain

and base metal? Today,
          I pin them on
                    my husband who seems

immobilized
          by my hands fumbling
                    not to hurt him,

the ribbons hard
          despite their apparent silk—
                    they don't bend

to fit the wearer,
          who is after all, part
                    of a vessel that is part

of a fleet in its gray deployments.
          Suppose for some there's peace
                    in these rows,

citations fit each to each,
          how every sacrifice already
                    knows its place.

CASUALTY NOTIFICATION

The Only News I know / Is Bulletins all Day /
From Immortality.
—Emily Dickinson

Switch channels, stop
    the breaking news,
press mute to hush
    the anchorman's reviews
of war, his litany
    of each device
and bomb gone off today.
    Silence the price
of bread or milk
    or gasoline.
Make the black pinpoint
    on the TV screen.
Unplug the black box
    from the mouth of the wall.
Uncradle the phone so
    nobody can call.
Let the venetian blinds
    blind everyone
to what's outside—the dead,
    indifferent sun,
the car pulled up along
    the curb, the vexed
men in uniforms
    looking for next
of kin. They bring a check
    to pay the cost
of grieving. Their dark sedan
    puffs out exhaust.
And now, the only sound
    a daybird singing,
the only bulletin
    a doorbell ringing

WAR WIDOW

She grieves like a woman repainting a room
that is too large, first arching to reach
the dark wall. When the roller can go no higher,

she climbs a ladder, stretching her arm
to the corners, dragging white Vs and Ws
as if trying to form words. She makes a fist

around the handle when her fingers go weak,
because clenching is better than stopping,
or else, picks up a brush, carves the line

of the ceiling until her wrist trembles
with the smallness of this work.
The edges filled in, she returns to the roller—

wide ribbons in paperwhite, whitewash,
seed pearl, or silver lining—trying to cover
every streak of shadow underneath.

THE LONG DEPLOYMENT

For weeks, I breathe his body in the sheet
        and pillow. I lift a blanket to my face.
There's bitter incense paired with something sweet,
        like sandalwood left sitting in the heat
or cardamom rubbed on a piece of lace.
        For weeks, I breathe his body. In the sheet
I smell anise, the musk that we secrete
        with longing, leather and moss. I find a trace
of bitter incense paired with something sweet.
        Am I imagining the wet scent of peat
and cedar, oud, impossible to erase?
        For weeks, I breathe his body in the sheet—
crushed pepper—although perhaps discreet,
        difficult for someone else to place.
There's bitter incense paired with something sweet.
        With each deployment I become an aesthete
of smoke and oak. Patchouli fills the space
        for weeks. I breathe his body in the sheet
until he starts to fade, made incomplete,
        a bottle almost empty in its case.
There's bitter incense paired with something sweet.
        And then he's gone. Not even the conceit
of him remains, not the resinous base.
        For weeks, I breathed his body in the sheet.
He was bitter incense paired with something sweet.

[IF YOU ARE SQUEAMISH]

Don't sift through shelves
in the officer's quarters,
or lift a blanket from the rack

to find a photograph
of a body split, splayed,
an article of clothing made

hard by longing. Don't scroll
his phone's green messages.
The ocean is another

water of forgetfulness.
Whatever washes up—
those things are rubble

on a beach. It's best to leave
some shells unlistened, some
shards of jaded glass unseen.

PHOTOGRAPH OF GENERAL PETRAEUS
WITH PAULA BROADWELL

later revealed to be his mistress

As with some painting from the Renaissance,
perspective pulls the eye to where his hand
encloses hers, his fingers reddening
around the white flesh of her palm. Notice
how even this professional touch has made
the General blush. He would do well to shun
a body pressed into a pencil skirt,
a bust that strains the limits of its blouse.
And yet the composition cannot work
without them both, their light a sweaty sheen.
He's dressed in green fatigues, four tiny stars
embroidered down the center of his shirt,
where underneath must lie his collarbone,
and on his sleeve, an eagle staring left,
away. We want to look away as well—
Petraeus from the ancient Greek for stone,
but here he's just a man, hardly alone
in wishing to unloop a silver hoop
from the velvet lobe of an ear, or let
the onyx bracelet fall beside a bed.
We scan the picture for intelligence.
The thick, expressive folds of national flags
are backdrop to the scene.

                    In Jan Van Eyck's
The Arnolfini Wedding, we can't stop
staring at the hands, her right outstretched
and resting in the cushion of his left.
They should be smiling, yet both seem staid
as if already they can sense the secrets
that weigh all unions with a dark brocade.
On the windowsill: a group of oranges
to signal wealth or else illicit fruit,
depending on which scholar we consult.
A broom. A bed. An amber rosary.

A dog who represents fidelity.
Behind the pair a convex mirror shows
what isn't shown—a door and witnesses,
the outside lookings of this little world.
How often do we watch two people stand
like this, held undistorted in the frame?
For a moment, we can see them as they are:
the woman cool, generic beauty; the man,
what hardness he contains now edged with longing.
All lines direct our gaze toward them, a glaze
of shadows, pale skin turned luminous,
the perfect clarity of their mistakes.

[LAMENT FOR THIS LONG CELIBACY]

—like a Pink Lady apple
left lying in a porcelain
plate on the countertop,

untouched at first
for the blush of its skin,
and later because who

would want such
over-ripening, juice
gone cider and flesh too

soft, as if even breath might
break it, not to mention
the white bite of teeth—

READING SAPPHO IN PENSACOLA

When you remember that summer,
you see the sweating hours—
                      how your fingers left

damp dimples in the pages
as if even reading produced too much heat
in the body; and the open minibar

        of your hotel room offered
the only breeze when you reached in
for another bottle.

It was always the afternoon that returned
                your husband to the door—
holding a map or a brochure,

some adventure to repair the fragments
of the day, a drive to the beach,
past titty-joints and pawnshops,

or if weather betrayed, a new book.
        In Pensacola, nothing
he brought made up for the morning,

his absence like the space
                a translator leaves
when only parts of the poem remain.

Looking back on that July, you can still
recite *a thin flame runs under my skin*,
still feel the wet washcloth laid

on your belly, anything to keep cool
                while you waited.
Sometimes, although you hated

        that sunburned strip of Florida,
watching gray geckos ascend the bathroom wall,
you could still be convinced to go back;

when he found you on the bed—
                    my tongue is broken,
you would say before proving yourself

a liar, not much broken then
but the ceiling fan that spun unsteady
circles, while the two of you slept, barely

wrapped in sheets the drifting color of sand.

PERSUASION

Surely Anne Elliot would understand
      words can be small ships of hope
or disappointment, that waiting is a choice, constancy
      like a rock toward which we leap,
Louisa Musgrove falling from the wall.
      When my husband calls
to say again his leave is cancelled or cut in half,
      I think of all those women by the sea—
their needlework and screens, their careful
      fingers on an instrument.
We none of us expect to be in smooth water all our days,
      says Mrs. Croft to Captain Wentworth,
who's convinced that wives belong on land
      or, if nothing else, confined
to narrow, rocking rooms. Elsewhere in the novel,
      Lady Russell says, *Time will explain,*
patience the usual hobby for fine ladies dressed in silks.
      We paint tiny portraits
of the ones deployed. We write riddles
      with the letters of their names.
I hate to be Anne Elliot, but I am.
      I will not allow books to prove anything,
she tells Captain Harville in chapter 23, who believes
      departure the difficult duty—
what a man suffers when he takes a last look at his wife.
      When my husband calls me
from the aircraft carrier, I think of all those women
      who *pay the tax of quick alarm.*
We persuade ourselves to love or not, persuade
      ourselves of the garden's beauty
and the walk alone through boxwood lanes, and the poem
      read for velvet cushions
undisturbed, still and empty audience of a chair.

ASKING AND TELLING

Desire revealed may never be erased.
  —Ovid, *Metamorphoses* 9.907

So carefully did no one touch,
    no chairs colliding, no cocktail sloshed
onto another's half-unbuttoned shirt,
     even the rings of water on the tabletop
kept separate and remote. My first night
    in the company of officers, they knocked back
drinks, each hand around a bottle's neck,
     the same mythology of manliness.
A rattlesnake, a jawbreaker, a sexy lemon slam.
    And when everyone else was drunk,
the jokes began: how do you separate
     the men from the boys in the Navy?—
with a crowbar and a bucket of cold water.
    And rhymes: it's only queer if you're tied
to the pier / it's not gay if you're underway.
     Someone sipped a slippery nipple. Someone
raised an amber glass to trap the light,
    the men's carved faces now beautiful with sweat.
And while I sat there saying nothing,
     mute as Psyche in the underworld—
already imagining the poem I could write—
    they told me it's don't ask, don't tell, and don't
pursue, sailors pried open of their secrets
     like unsealing a box that's rusted shut.
Another round of shots and then another.
     Someone ordered a pearl necklace,
someone a sit on my face, a horny bull,
    a snakebite. Pursuit, they said, can also mean
the chasing of desire, that certain longings
     should be stopped with lead arrows
to the heart. Or like mortals hunted
    by insatiate gods, some must run from the heat
of their own bodies, must turn
     to laurels in a forest thick with silences
where everything keeps gulping down the rain.

THE BEAUFORT SCALE

Because the wind is hard to quantify—
a thing invisible itself—we must
assess the wind by what it does, each gust
a consequence across the sea and sky:
that *calm* is mirrorlike, *light air* a sigh
that barely moves the waves, *strong breezes* thrust,
make whitecaps, and crests of foam imply
near gale or *storm* or *hurricane*. We trust
our eyes. We understand how feelings change
like weather troubling the surface of
the sea. We see our feelings in the surges
they create, the way they rearrange
the ocean of ourselves, that this is love—
these breaks and swells, these spindrift urges.

ELEGY WITH FULL DRESS BLUES

Early in our marriage I would stand
    at the edge
of his closet like a visitor
    at a planetarium,
often only a finger lifted toward the bright
    lacing at the sleeve or the stars
in their glinting thread
    and pretend that all
this fabric was a well-constructed sky,
    night made orderly
as a row of brass buttons,
    on nearby hangers shirts glowing
the same white
    as some precise and flattened moon,
which almost I could touch,
    if not for the worry
of wrinkling, and the satin
    cummerbund that bounded the evening
in an ellipse
    the size of a waist,
although it was polyester and more yellow
    than gold, and the gilded
studs at the wrists not genuine points
    of safety but paste, the dusky
lacquer of his plastic shoes,
    and most of all pairs of opaque gloves
laid out on a tray, pale series
    of consequential hands,
their tips a little smudged
    and gesturing
at a darker hour I could almost see.

ARMED SERVICES EDITIONS

pocket-size paperbacks published during
World War II for soldiers overseas

My copy of *The Fireside Book of Verse*
is as the seller promised—the stapled spine,
the paper aged to Army tan—no worse
for wear, given the cost of its design,
six cents to make and printed on a press
once used for magazines and pulp. This book
was never meant to last a war much less
three quarters of a century.
                              I look
for evidence of all the men who scanned
these lines, crouched down in holes or lying in
their racks. I read the poems secondhand.
Someone has creased a page. Did he begin
then stop to sleep? to clean his gun perhaps?
to listen to the bugler playing taps?

LIBERTY

Tomorrow he would leave again
and I thought why not
remove his clothes once more,
fold his shirt in the familiar ceremony
of undress. I tugged a button
from its hole as if opening
had always been this easy.
I hurried my fingers to his collarbone
where I once imagined a thread
could unravel the tight symbols tied
inside of him. We were following
the line of dropping clothes
when he pulled away to touch the cover
draped across the bed, rows
of fabric I had pieced together,
small imperfect stars. I believed
in the seam our bodies made,
but when in the morning he put on
his uniform, it was what I'd sewn
myself that held, miraculous,
our warmth—his face now a pattern
indecipherable if viewed up close.
And even at a distance, I couldn't
pick out more than his blurring
shape, a vague field of color,
those strips of ribbon at his chest.

NOTES

Poems in this book were written in conversation with works by W. H. Auden, Jane Austen, Mary Barnard (her *Sappho: A New Translation*), Raymond Carver, Stephen Crane, Emily Dickinson, Mark Doty, Jack Gilbert, Robert Hayden, Mark Irwin, Brigit Pegeen Kelly, A. E. Stallings, Kurt Vonnegut, and Bruce Weigl.

"Runaway Military Surveillance Blimp Drifts from Maryland to Pennsylvania" takes its title from a *New York Times* article.

Phrases from "Patton" echo passages in George S. Patton's speech to the Third Army on June 5, 1944.

As referenced in "The Beaufort Scale," the Beaufort Wind Force Scale, created in 1805 by Sir France Beaufort of the British Royal Navy, measures wind speed by observing its effects on the sea and on land.

ACKNOWLEDGMENTS

My gratitude to the editors of the publications in which some of these poems first appeared:

Academy of American Poets, Poem-a-Day Program:
     "Homeport" and "The Long Deployment"
Bellevue Literary Review: "Armed Services Editions"
Blackbird: "November 11"
Collateral: "Patton" and "Tackle Box"
Construction: "A Catalogue of the Contents of His Nightstand,"
     "Liberty," and "My Husband Calls Me Shipmate"
Copper Nickel: "SOS"
Crab Orchard Review: "[To a Navy Wife, in Maryland]"
Crazyhorse: "From the Aberdeen Proving Ground"
Ecotone: "From the Pentagon"
Iron Horse Literary Review: "[The Dependent Says]" and "[If
     You Are Squeamish]"
Mid-American Review: "What We Talk about When We Talk
     about Deployment"
New England Review: "Reading Sappho in Pensacola"
North Dakota Quarterly: "CAUTION: HOLE IN SHIP" and
     "Photograph of General Petraeus with Paula Broadwell"
Plume: "Elegy with Full Dress Blues"
Salamander: "At the Reading of the Antiwar Poets, 2007"
Southeast Review: "Asking and Telling"
Tupelo Quarterly: "USS *Ronald Reagan*"
Verse Daily: "Casualty Notification"
War, Literature, and the Arts: "Five Poetry Readings,"
     "Ramrod," and "A Row of Ribbons"
West Branch: "Casualty Notification" and "Reading Poetry on
     Maryland Public Radio"
Witness: "[Then the God of War]"

"Armed Services Editions" was featured as newspaper column no.
553 in Ted Kooser's *American Life in Poetry*.
     "A Catalogue of the Contents of His Nightstand" appeared in
Still Life with Poem: Contemporary Natures Mortes in Verse (Literary
House Press, 2016).

"The Long Deployment" appeared in *Poem-a-Day: 365 Poems for Every Occasion* (Abrams, 2015) and in *The Book of Scented Things: 100 Contemporary Poems about Perfume* (Literary House Press, 2014). This poem was also turned into a film by video artist Nicole McDonald of Psyop for the sixth season of Motionpoems.

The first section of "Much Tattooed Sailor aboard USS *New Jersey*" was written for National Archives Month; the poem was featured on the websites of the National Archives and the Academy of American Poets.